YOUR KNOWLEDGE HAS VALUE

Implications of Outsourcing in IT-Management

GRIN ☺

Bibliographic information published by the German National Library:

The German National Library lists this publication in the National Bibliography; detailed bibliographic data are available on the Internet at http://dnb.dnb.de.

ISBN: 9783346566119
This book is also available as an ebook.

© GRIN Publishing GmbH
Nymphenburger Straße 86
80636 München

Print and binding: Books on Demand GmbH, Norderstedt, Germany
Printed on acid-free paper from responsible sources.

The present work has been carefully prepared. Nevertheless, authors and publishers do not incur liability for the correctness of information, notes, links and advice as well as any printing errors.

GRIN web shop: https://www.grin.com/document/1152718

term paper

part-time degree program
4. Semester
in the study course Wirtschaftsinformatik

in the context of the course
IT-Management

on the subject

Implications of Outsourcing in IT-Management

Contents

One illustration has been removed from this paper!

List of Figures

List of Tables

List of Abbreviations

IaaS	Infrastructure as a Service
PaaS	Platform as a Service
RFI	Request for Information
RFP	Request for Proposal
SaaS	Software as a Service
TCO	Total Cost of Ownership

1 Introduction

This paper takes a closer look at aspects surrounding the importance and application of IT outsourcing and aims to provide a sound understanding of the term as well as the forms of outsourcing strategy in today's IT-based or IT-driven industries. Since outsourcing is a subject that is not necessarily only associated with advantages, a closer look at the disadvantages of outsourcing will also be taken in the course of this paper.

1.1 Actuality and Importance of Outsourcing

Outsourcing has become increasingly popular as a technique to reduce costs and to access a wider range of technical expertise (in-house competencies versus outsourcing non-core competencies).[1] Especially concerning the second example, outsourcing has become a standard method of project and labor management if a firm decides to migrate to a newer technology.[2] In the IT industry, companies may outsource system development, system operations, help desk, systems, databases, and application administration, as well as a desktop and network support. Furthermore, businesses may use outsourcing to obtain application service provision or business process outsourcing.[3]

Figure 1: Typical outsourcing candidates

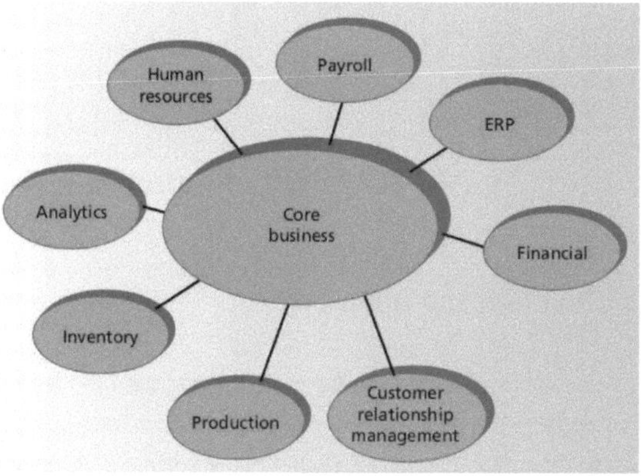

Quelle: *Laplante, P.* et al., The who, what, why, where, and when of IT outsourcing, 2004, S. 21

---

[1] Vgl. *Vorontsova, A., Rusu, L.*, Determinants of IT Outsourcing Relationships, 2014, S. 589.
[2] Vgl. *Vorontsova, A., Rusu, L.*, Determinants of IT Outsourcing Relationships, 2014, S. 589.
[3] Vgl. *Vorontsova, A., Rusu, L.*, Determinants of IT Outsourcing Relationships, 2014, S. 589.

Considering an IT activity a commodity, there is little benefit to doing it internally. Payroll processing, for instance, is often considered a commodity IT activity. In these cases, focused vendors are likely capable of providing the service at a higher level of quality and/or at a lower cost. By taking advantage of economies of scale that other organizations have, a business that specializes in the same field can become more cost-effective.[4] With respect to the given advantages outsourcing of IT resources and services is proving to be an increasing trend on the global market. Companies such as cloud providers specializing in many different manifestations of IT outsourcing (Infrastructure as a Service (IaaS), Platform as a Service (PaaS), Software as a Service (SaaS)) show a growing turnover, which is expected to increase further in the forecast beyond 2021.

Figure 2: Public cloud revenue by segment

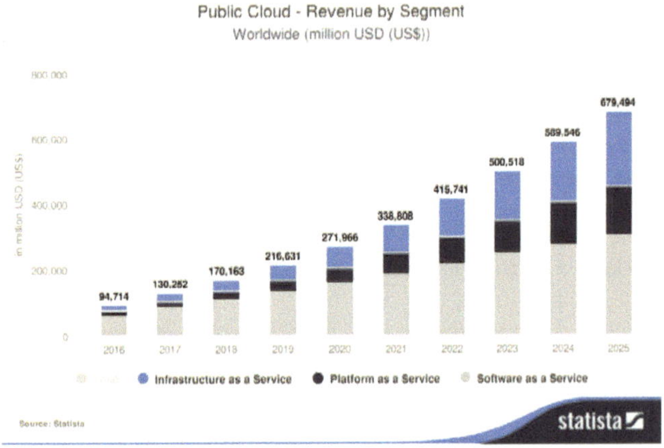

Source: *Statista*, Public Cloud Revenue by Segment, 2021

1.2 Structure and Approach

This study is divided into two parts. In the first part, the term outsourcing is explained in more detail and a deeper understanding of the characteristics, applications and development of the methodology is acquired.In the second part, potential risks and opportunities of IT outsourcing are discussed. The summary takes a final look at what has been learned so far about the methodology and the resulting conclusions.

---

[4] Vgl. *Laplante, P.* et al., The who, what, why, where, and when of IT outsourcing, 2004, S. 21.

2 Fundamentals of Outsourcing

2.1 Definition

Since the emergence of a productivity-oriented economy, not only has competition become established, but economic cooperation opportunities between market participants have also developed to generate competitive advantages. In this context, the consideration of outsourcing service parts to professional subcontractors or partners is also playing an increasingly important role. These first "make-or-buy" decisions marked the beginning of classic outsourcing. Hardly any other industry produces as many buzzwords as the information technology industry. For those directly involved, but even more so for customers and potential users, the problem arises of finding one's way through this jungle. Thus, several definitions exist for the term "outsourcing", which is a compound of the nouns "outside", "resource" and "using". Literally translated, outsourcing means "using resources from outside". Outsourcing generally means the outsourcing of certain partial services or functions of a company and their takeover by third-party service providers. In this context, it is irrelevant whether the services or production processes are involved and whether the services were formerly created internally or newly integrated.[5]

2.2 Historical Development of the Idea of Outsourcing and its Concept

Although outsourcing is often marketed as the newest strategic management tool, it has been around for years. It is not possible to pinpoint the exact time of its emergence. The first documented use dates back to 1954, when General Electric collaborated with Arthur Andersen and Univac in the area of information systems.[6]

Rising to this, outsourcing developed into a significant economic factor by the early 1980s. This resulted from the fact that many industries, faced with increasing cost pressure, outsourced their cost-intensive production processes to so-called "low-wage countries" in Southeast Asia. The cost pressure was so strong that it was worthwhile to manufacture in another country with lower production costs and ship the finished product halfway around the world. Outsourcing production facilities increased administrative costs enormously. Accordingly, production was no longer carried out at just one location but, if necessary, at several locations on several continents. In order to cope with the resulting enormous

---

[5] cf. *Hagen, R., Stefan, D., Kai T., B.*, IT-Outsourcing, 2013, p. 2f.
[6] cf. *Walters, B., Tang, Z.*, IT-Enabled Strategic Management, 2006, p. 247.

administrative workload, the company made use of the constantly developing information and communication technology. Information and communication technology enabled the mass processing of large amounts of data, giving IT-supported companies a significant advantage. Due to the aforementioned cost pressure and competition on the market, almost all companies, especially small and medium-sized ones, were encouraged to invest more in their own IT. The fact that the core competencies of these companies are usually not IT-related encouraged the willingness to outsource in these areas. The American company Eastman Kodak was the first to outsource its entire IT system in 1989. As a result of this outsourcing, the company was able to reduce its IT costs by almost 20%.[7]

In the 1990s, there was a renewed interest in outsourcing and the strategic use of outsourcing. There were two different purposes. First, the interest in outsourcing was to reduce staff in order to save costs, generate a competitive advantage and keep the company lean. Next, due to the technical advancement of programming languages, was to upgrade legacy systems from 3rd generation to 4th generation. This was not possible for many companies due to lack of know-how and human resources. These lacking resources were to be purchased or the upgrade outsourced, to ensure a smooth transition. In 1999, on-site facility management and selective outsourcing increased in outsourcing, especially in areas related to the Y2K problem (i.e. the millennium bug). This is reflected in the use of temporary workers and the first application of offshore outsourcing, particularly in India.[8]

Since the 2000s, the term outsourcing has not changed much. In recent years, the focus has been increasingly on the areas of business process outsourcing and offshore outsourcing. Business processes that are outsourced serve to redefine the internal structure of a company. Here, the focus of a company is on outsourcing administration, transactions and similar tasks in order to save costs and gain access to new technologies. Furthermore, outsourcing is intended to focus on strategic issues of a company. Nowadays, we are essentially talking about services that the outsourcing provider takes over. One service, for example, consists of outsourcing complete defined business processes to external service providers who manage them. This is to ensure complete integration between the outsourced business processes and the internal processes.[9]

2.3 Forms of Integration and Possibilities in Outsourcing

Outsourcing only means in exceptional cases that companies free themselves from the entire tasks of, for example, IT. Rather, the aim is to obtain those services from outside which

---

[7] cf. *Hagen, R., Stefan, D., Kai T., B.*, IT-Outsourcing, 2013, p. 2f.

[8] cf. *Walters, B., Tang, Z.*, IT-Enabled Strategic Management, 2006, p. 248.

[9] cf. *Walters, B., Tang, Z.*, IT-Enabled Strategic Management, 2006, p. 248.

external providers can provide or handle more efficiently. In other words, it is a question of the appropriateness of inter-and intra-company division of labor or optimization of service depth. In this context, it should be noted that in the case of service depth optimization, a decision must be made not only between the two alternatives "pure in-house production" and "pure external procurement", but also that a number of institutional forms of integration are possible for internal management.[10] Outsourcing can be divided into two meanings. On the one hand, outsourcing can be understood as the outsourcing of IT services to external companies or external service providers. On the other hand, outsourcing can be understood as the transfer of the IT department to an independent or non-independent organization. If only a partial area or a partial task of company activities is outsourced, this is referred to as partial or selective outsourcing. If the outsourcing customer wants to outsource its entire IT operations or large parts (tasks) of its IT operations, but does not want to place these in the hands of an outsourcing provider in the sense of total outsourcing, but instead outsources them to different service providers, this is referred to as multisourcing or multi-vendor outsourcing. With a multisourcing strategy, the outsourcing customer uses not just one service provider but many different outsourcing providers who, as individual entrepreneurs, have specialized in a particular IT area. A major disadvantage of multisourcing is the interfaces between the individual outsourcing providers.[11]

In total or complete outsourcing, the majority of a group's or company's IT activities are performed by an external service provider (outsourcing provider). This economic process is referred to in different ways, but as result it is the same process.[12]
Business process outsourcing refers to a business relationship in which a provider takes over a complete business process or corporate function, including all the information technology that supports it. In contrast to conventional outsourcing, the provider is free in the technical implementation. The customer obtains the process result without being involved in the area of responsibility or the data processing infrastructure.[13]

2.4 IT services and their Possibility for Outsourcing

IT outsourcing describes the external procurement of IT services such as functions and processes. Information processing generally affects all of a company's processes and thus assumes a central cross-sectional function. If this cross-sectional function fails over a longer period of time, the core business may come to a standstill and the company can no

[10] cf. *Picot, A., Maier, M.*, Anaylse- und Gestaltungskonzepte für das Outsourcing, 1993, p. 20.
[11] cf. *Söbbing, T.*, Handbuch IT-Outsourcing, 2002, p. 47.
[12] cf. *Söbbing, T.*, Handbuch IT-Outsourcing, 2002, p. 33.
[13] cf. *Söbbing, T.*, Handbuch IT-Outsourcing, 2002, p. 49.

longer fulfill its original purpose. Information processing is thus closely intertwined with the core business and assumes a central and essential role. Outsourcing, in the information processing industry, is therefore much more complex than in comparison with a classic supplier company.[14]

Table 1: Forms of IT Outsourcing

Professional Services	System Integration	Facility Management
IT consulting	User support	Data center
System development	Desktop Management	Handing over overall responsibility to outsourcing providers
System design	Network infrastructure	
Installation	Network operation	
Software development	Disaster preparedness	
Programming	Large system applications	
Training		

source based on *Lux, W., Schön, P.*, Outsourcing der Datenverarbeitung, 2012, p. 4-6

Professional Service describes the external implementation of IT projects outside the company. As shown in the Table 1, classic IT services are offered e.g. IT consulting and System development. Here, the outsourcing provider is only liable for solution responsibility and is detached from financial responsibility. Usually, short- to medium-term individual contracts are signed.[15]

System Integration expands Professional Services. New complex solutions were created, such as user support, network operation, large-scale system applications, or even the transfer of employees to outsourcing companies. These new solutions use and rely on hardware, software, network, and professional services and thus represent new outsourcing opportunities.[16]

Outsourcing in facility management represents the classic form of outsourcing. Here, the outsourcing provider takes over partial areas or the entire information processing. In this case, the provider takes over all employees, operational and financial responsibility for the general contractor. In principle, contractual arrangements are concluded over a long period of time. System management is a further development of facility management and includes the strategic responsibility for information processing. This gives rise to risks for the outsourcer, as it has to delimit the IT services that still have to be provided itself.[17]

---

[14] cf. *Lux, W., Schön, P.*, Outsourcing der Datenverarbeitung, 2012, p. 4-6.
[15] cf. *Lux, W., Schön, P.*, Outsourcing der Datenverarbeitung, 2012, p. 4.
[16] cf. *Lux, W., Schön, P.*, Outsourcing der Datenverarbeitung, 2012, p. 5.
[17] cf. *Lux, W., Schön, P.*, Outsourcing der Datenverarbeitung, 2012, p. 6.

2.5 Phases of Outsourcing

Outsourcing IT services is not a one-off action, but a process consisting of several phases. General recommendations for action are hardly possible here. In contrast, analysis schemes and assessment frameworks which focus attention on the factors relevant to the decision and provide tools for decision support prove to be very helpful.

Figure 3: IT outsourcing lifecycle

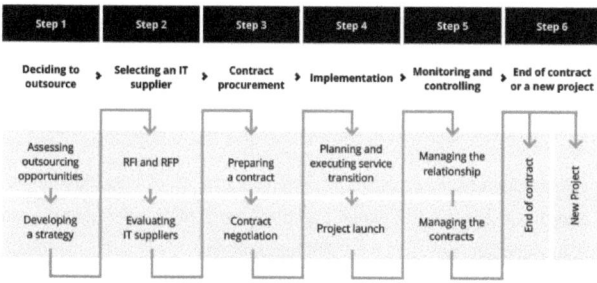

cf. *Future Processing Start Nearshoring*, IT outsourcing lifecycle, 2021

Figure 3 shows the complex outsourcing process. The outsourcing process can be divided into six steps. These steps are each subdivided into subphases or subprocesses. In this way, a systematic, methodical approach can be achieved. The first step is to identify potential opportunities for outsourcing. In this step a strategy is designed. This often involves a comprehensive target-performance analysis of the existing IT structure, followed by a Total Cost of Ownership (TCO) analysis of the corresponding costs for business and IT processes.[18] The next step is the selection of IT suppliers. Here the Request for Information (RFI) and the Request for Proposal (RFP) play an important role. An RFI is designed to collect information from a supplier or vendor with no commitment to engage in any particular project. The RFP focuses on specifying a scope of work that needs to be performed (the RFP) and solicits in response a Proposal from the vendor describing how they would go about executing the project – including pricing information. The next step is to negotiate the contract. Continuing, the implementation begins, where the planning and executing service transition and the project launch is done.[19] The next step is monitoring

---

[18] cf. *Söbbing, T.*, Handbuch IT-Outsourcing, 2002, p. 65.
[19] cf. *Söbbing, T.*, Handbuch IT-Outsourcing, 2002, p. 98.

and controlling, where the relationships and contracts are maintained. The end of the IT outsourcing lifecycle describes the end of the project or the beginning of a new project.[20]

3 Motivation and Risks of IT-Outsourcing

The outsourcing of IT services of a company can have various reasons, which are expected to have positive effects. However, there are also risks and negative side effects that can hinder such a project or make it unprofitable for the company. In the following, not only the the chances of IT outsourcing are explained, but also the risks are pointed out.

3.1 Chances of Outsourcing

A distinction between strategic, financial and other opportunities is made in order to evaluate the subject with several perspectives. These will now be examined in more detail to help illustrate the chances of IT-Outsourcing.

3.1.1 Strategic Chances

Improvement of flexibility: One chance that results from outsourcing is that the resources that are required for an IT service are more flexible. A project, technology or platform needs different amounts of resources like personnel over its lifetime.[21] Dynamic resource management of this kind arises from changes to the requirements of the service or, in some cases, from changing or merging platforms and systems. These changes are essential to remain profitable and to maintain a competitive advantage.[22] Through outsourcing, for example, the workforce that is required can be changed dynamically without employees having to be newly hired or dismissed. This means that you are independent of staff shortages or overhangs and the ability to react to new requirements is massively improved.[23]

Risk transfer: Another opportunity for the company is the transfer of risk to the outsource service provider. In this case, the service provider not only bears the cost risk, but also the risk regarding quality and personnel responsibility.[24] This leads to more stable financial

---

[20] cf. *Söbbing, T.*, Handbuch IT-Outsourcing, 2002, p. 177.
[21] cf. *Amberg, M., Wiener, M.*, IT-Offshoring, 2006, p. 44f.
[22] cf. *Beulen, E., Ribbers, P., Roos, J.*, Managing IT Outsourcing, 2006, p. 15.
[23] cf. *Amberg, M., Wiener, M.*, IT-Offshoring, 2006, p. 44f.
[24] cf. *Schwarze, L., Müller, P.*, IT-Outsourcing – Erfahrungen, 2005, p. 9.

planning and defines a clear structure of who is held accountable. Because if the service provider cannot fulfill the agreements, he has to accept a penalty and therefore takes over the responsibility.[25] Furthermore, risk management involves resource-intensive research about the market and how it is changed by financial, political or technical influences. Since the service provider has already gained a lot of experience in the market, he can assess possible risks particularly well and adapt to them.[26]

Concentration on the core business: In most companies, many IT services are not part of the core business. They are often only supportive and have little direct added value for the product.[27] For this reason, these non-core competencies are often outsourced in order to be able to use the freed-up resources in the core business and gain a competitive advantage. Which IT services are part of the core business and which are not must be decided individually and depends on the relevance to the core business processes.[28] In addition, it is possible to select specific services that are particularly resource-intensive or have caused problems in the past. This allows the company to focus on the problems, business goals and customer requirements of the main business.[29] In general, it can be said that processes become simpler and require less coordination. This more flexible way of working allows bottlenecks to be avoided and the main business to be driven forward.[30]

Company restructuring: The strategic tools of a company also include the restructuring of the company and its departments. Such restructurings are very complex, especially in IT, and must be perfectly executed to enable collaboration.[31] Restructuring can mean realigning, selling or even merging both internal or external departments or companies. Outsourcing simplifies such processes because the IT can be adapted to the situation more quickly. In the course of restructuring, it is also often examined whether the services belong to the core business and how the performance of the internal department compares to possible outsourcing offers.[32]

Up to date with the latest technological developments: Information technologies are in a constant state of change. They are becoming more and more complex and require many resources to be kept up to date.[33] But also the introduction of new applications and platforms is a challenge for companies, because the necessary know-how and investment

---

[25] cf. *Amberg, M., Wiener, M.,* IT-Offshoring, 2006, p. 47f.
[26] cf. *Walters, B., Tang, Z.,* IT-Enabled Strategic Management, 2006, p. 253.
[27] cf. *Amberg, M., Wiener, M.,* IT-Offshoring, 2006, p. 45f.
[28] cf. *Schwarze, L., Müller, P.,* IT-Outsourcing – Erfahrungen, 2005, p. 9.
[29] cf. *Walters, B., Tang, Z.,* IT-Enabled Strategic Management, 2006, p. 252.
[30] cf. *Deering, A.,* Outsourcing, 2015, p. 46.
[31] cf. *Beulen, E., Ribbers, P., Roos, J.,* Managing IT Outsourcing, 2006, p. 16.
[32] cf. *Amberg, M., Wiener, M.,* IT-Offshoring, 2006, p. 46.
[33] cf. *Beulen, E., Ribbers, P., Roos, J.,* Managing IT Outsourcing, 2006, p. 15f.

is needed. Here, outsourcing is a more cost-effective alternative, as not only does the service provider implement the latest system, but also operates both systems simultaneously during implementation, thus promising a seamless transition.[34]

Reducing time-to-market: A shorter time-to-market makes it possible to adapt more quickly to new circumstances and thus significantly increases a company's competitive advantage. Especially in software development, implementation and technical support, the principle of "follow-the-sun" can create efficient resource management. By offshoring parts of the workload, the time zone advantage can be exploited, and a project can be continued almost seamlessly overnight. An example of this would be when a software company in the US decides to move some of their development to India in order to use cheaper labor overnight due to the large time difference of almost 12 hours.[35] Other possibilities to reduce the time-to-market would be on the one hand a central portal for the exchange of information, which is also essential for the principle "follow-the-sun" and on the other hand the consideration if a customized solution is needed or if the faster standard solution is sufficient in which the outsourcing service provider could already gain experience.[36]

3.1.2 Financial Chances

Reducing costs: One of the main motives why companies outsource is to achieve cost savings, especially in the operational area. These result from several influences. On the one hand, service providers can exploit their size advantage and specialization to obtain better hardware and software prices.[37] On the other hand, there are also major cost benefits from taking advantage of lower labor and ancillary costs when offshoring.[38] The literature estimates potential cost savings from outsourcing of 17 to 40 percent. However, this depends on many different factors, which must be reassessed in each company's initial situation and must be well planned. These include, for example, the scope of the outsourcing, that means whether only one application or the entire infrastructure is outsourced.[39,40,41,42]

Fixed cost conversion: IT costs are primarily fixed costs, such as personnel or material costs. If demand increases, IT capacities must be built up, which represents a burden for

[34] cf. *Amberg, M., Wiener, M.,* IT-Offshoring, 2006, p. 46f.
[35] cf. *Djavanshir, G.,* Surveying the risks and benefits of IT outsourcing, 2005, p. 34.
[36] cf. *Beulen, E., Ribbers, P., Roos, J.,* Managing IT Outsourcing, 2006, p. 14f.
[37] cf. *Deering, A.,* Outsourcing, 2015, p. 45f.
[38] cf. *Amberg, M., Wiener, M.,* IT-Offshoring, 2006, p. 39f.
[39] cf. *Walters, B., Tang, Z.,* IT-Enabled Strategic Management, 2006, p. 252.
[40] cf. *Amberg, M., Wiener, M.,* IT-Offshoring, 2006, p. 39f.
[41] cf. *Schwarze, L., Müller, P.,* IT-Outsourcing – Erfahrungen, 2005, p. 8f.
[42] cf. *Djavanshir, G.,* Surveying the risks and benefits of IT outsourcing, 2005, p. 33.

the company if demand decreases again. Companies that have strong fluctuations in their IT requirements are particularly affected by this.[43] Outsourcing can transform fixed costs into variable costs if a consumption-based pricing model has been agreed with the service provider beforehand. In this way, the problem of fixed costs can be prevented or solved, especially if the employees are also outsourced.[44] The outsourcing service provider does not have the problem of fixed costs, since he can use the resources flexibly for different customers.[45]

Reduction of capital commitment: Another financial advantage is the reduced capital commitment. Since assets such as servers and desktops are carried by the service provider, companies improve there liquidity.[46] This means that the capital that is actually tied up can be invested in other areas, such as activities that are of greater strategic importance. In addition, existing assets can be sold to the service provider to obtain a certain liquidity effect.[47]

3.1.3 Other Definable Opportunities

Access to technical know-how and qualified workforce: Another significant advantage of outsourcing is the utilization of the service provider's know-how. The service provider sells not only a service, but also access to his know-how. Through the enriched expert knowledge of the provider, which he has acquired through cooperation with other companies with similar challenges, the own company benefits without having to make time and cost-intensive training or hire specialized IT experts.[48] This can result in better service quality or even a competitive advantage.[49] This know-how becomes particularly important when it comes to special topics, which occur more frequently in IT due to increasingly complex interrelationships.[50] Furthermore, outsourcing solves the problem of lack of qualified personnel. IT experts are in high demand and companies have to be attractive for employees. Outsourcing service providers are very attractive in this respect, because they offer a lot of training and have varied subject areas.[51] In addition, offshore outsourcing opens up a new labor market in which many well-trained workers and talents can be utilized.[52]

---

[43] cf. *Amberg, M., Wiener, M.,* IT-Offshoring, 2006, p. 41.
[44] cf. *Schwarze, L., Müller, P.,* IT-Outsourcing – Erfahrungen, 2005, p. 8.
[45] cf. *Beulen, E., Ribbers, P., Roos, J.,* Managing IT Outsourcing, 2006, p. 18.
[46] cf. *Amberg, M., Wiener, M.,* IT-Offshoring, 2006, p. 41f.
[47] cf. *Schwarze, L., Müller, P.,* IT-Outsourcing – Erfahrungen, 2005, p. 8.
[48] cf. *Amberg, M., Wiener, M.,* IT-Offshoring, 2006, p. 43f.
[49] cf. *Walters, B., Tang, Z.,* IT-Enabled Strategic Management, 2006, p. 252.
[50] cf. *Schwarze, L., Müller, P.,* IT-Outsourcing – Erfahrungen, 2005, p. 9.
[51] cf. *Beulen, E., Ribbers, P., Roos, J.,* Managing IT Outsourcing, 2006, p. 21.
[52] cf. *Djavanshir, G.,* Surveying the risks and benefits of IT outsourcing, 2005, p. 33.

3.2 Risks of Outsourcing

There are many advantages to outsourcing in IT-related areas, as can be seen from the examples above. But as with any strategic or financial methodology, there are certain risks and limitations that always need to be considered when deciding between a make or buy approach.

3.2.1 Strategic Risks

Knowledge drain: A frequently mentioned risk related to the use of outsourcing concerns the loss of organizational competencies, thereby increasing the dependency on external service providers. Since outsourcing arrangements often involve the transfer of workforce, a company's internal expertise can be significantly reduced. The knowledge required for setting up, developing and operating systems is wide-ranging, especially in the domain of IT.[53] To reduce the loss of internal expertise, which in turn impacts organizational competencies, companies should undertake a in-depth evaluation of all employees prior to a corporate transition in order to identify staff that needs to be retained based on the skills required.[54]

Lock-in: Lock-in is a risk that builds upon the previously mentioned risk of knowledge drain. A lock-in situation can occur when a company has not retained enough in-house expertise or when there are only a few service providers capable of providing the breadth and depth of services required. Contractual and practical safeguards, such as strategic partnerships based on risk sharing and mutual goals, and dual sourcing strategies involving the use of multiple service providers, are required to mitigate lock-in. Some companies, such as British Aerospace, have purposefully retained control of strategic IT functions in order to avoid lock-in.[55]

Concentration risks: The increasing dependence on the single leading firms e.g. in the cloud services domain may result in so called concentration risks. Amazon and Google offer cloud infrastructures and platforms which are linked to numerous other cloud services. Hence a whole ecosystem of services, including the clients, is damaged if such core infrastructure breaks down.[56] A company that relies on the outsourcing of IT services

---

[53] cf. *Georg Hodosi, L. R.*, Risks, Relationships and Success Factors in IT Outsourcing, 2019, p. 11-12.

[54] cf. *Walters, B., Tang, Z.*, IT-Enabled Strategic Management, 2006, p. 253.

[55] cf. *Walters, B., Tang, Z.*, IT-Enabled Strategic Management, 2006, p. 254.

[56] cf. *Hirschheim, R., Heinzl, A., Dibbern, J.*, Information Systems Outsourcing, 2020, p. 13f.

and tasks can hardly protect itself against this risk. Conversely, this means that when selecting a cloud provider, for example, it is particularly important to pay attention to the contractually regulated compensation in the event of incidents and system failures.

Reduction in quality of service: Any reduction in the quality of service received by a customer is referred to as service degradation. The quality of service may deteriorate over the course of the contract or simply fall below the agreed-upon level. This can be mitigated by making good use of service level agreements.[57] Organizations must be able to evaluate the performance of outsourced services in order for any implementation to be successful. A classic example for outsourceable units with high requirements may be the outsourcing of software development teams. Particularly in software development, aspects such as good code quality, interoperability with internal systems, the possibility of quick-changes, code documentation and traceability are of prime importance throughout the entire project life-cycle. If a company lacks the skills needed to understand and track these concepts, it is unclear whether the performance of the development teams is sufficient to keep up with the standards of other companies and customers.[58]

Communicative implications: Communication is key when it comes to planning and executing on outsourcing-relationships.[59] Greater distances between service supplier and buyer decrease both effectiveness and efficiency of communication. If the two firms are separated by numerous time zones and have only a few shared office hours, seemingly insignificant activities like phone conversations might become a primary challenge. Another concern may be a difference in nationality and language: Unless both parties speak the same native language, at least one must negotiate in a foreign language. The quality of communication may deteriorate depending on linguistic proficiency. Expensive and difficult communication might simply result in less communication, which can lead to a breakdown in management quality. Given the risks of communication costs, in the first outcome of a potential offshore scenario the customer is advised to consider communication costs carefully. This applies especially if the projects are likely, such as innovative products (and/or new technologies), to have extensive communication needs.[60]

[57] cf. *Aubert, B.* et al., Managing the risk of IT outsourcing, 1999, p. 1f.
[58] cf. *Walters, B., Tang, Z.,* IT-Enabled Strategic Management, 2006, p. 253.
[59] cf. *Georg Hodosi, L. R.,* Risks, Relationships and Success Factors in IT Outsourcing, 2019, p. 33.
[60] cf. *Rost, J.,* The Insider's Guide to Outsourcing Risks and Rewards, 2006, p. 133.

3.2.2 Financial Risks

Cost escalation: Cost escalation can occur as a result of unexpected expenses that cause an overrun of the original contracted estimates. This includes developing and maintaining an exchange relationship, monitoring exchange behavior (e.g., monitoring service levels), and hedging against opportunism. This can be mitigated by conducting a thorough financial analysis prior to outsourcing and utilizing definitive service level agreements that clearly define the financial basis and terms of the outsourcing arrangement.[61] Costs incurred for a cloud-hosted system, for example, which initially appear to be affordable and inviting, can increase rapidly and unexpectedly as the number of users and workload increase. Especially for externally hosted systems, it is therefore advisable to calculate resource utilization scenarios in advance.[62]

3.2.3 Other Definable Risks

Political risk factors through offshoring: Depending on its characteristics, the political situation within an external country can have a particularly strong influence on the benefits of offshoring. Offshore outsourcing may expose firms to the dangers of political unrest and instability, wars, seizures, nationalizations, and terrorism, as well as government laws, regulations, and potentially hostile government attitudes toward international enterprises. Political risk can have a financial impact on businesses due to interruptions in the continuity of company operations. Government regulations and policies in some developing countries can change abruptly (and often arbitrarily) based on individual decisions made by heads of state. To overcome this challenge, researcher Barry C. Lynn, a fellow at the New American Foundation, a public policy institute, suggests that businesses are required to diversify their economic activity across borders.[63]

Information vulnerability and security: There is increasing evidence that the externalization of IT-related activities may contribute significantly to cyber security issues. Recent examples include the multi-hour Salesforce Cloud crash owing to a flaw in the database that allowed non-administrative users to gain access to private data (May 2019):

---

[61] cf. *Walters, B., Tang, Z.*, IT-Enabled Strategic Management, 2006, p. 253.
[62] cf. *Hirschheim, R., Heinzl, A., Dibbern, J.*, Information Systems Outsourcing, 2020, p. 320-328.
[63] cf. *Djavanshir, G.*, Surveying the risks and benefits of IT outsourcing, 2005, p. 35.

Figure 4: Salesforce database incident

This illustration has been removed

Source: *CNBC*, Salesforces 'major issue' with its cloud service, 2019

Outages and security problems like these are not uncommon, even with large cloud providers.[64] Similar incidents include the large data breach for Capital One (an american banking company) caused by a former Amazon Cloud Services employee who extracted sensitive information from over 100 million customer accounts, hosted on intentionally misconfigured Amazon-Servers (July 2019) and the cloud breakdown for Google which struck platforms like YouTube, Gmail and Snapchat throughout the US (June 2019).[65] Offshore outsourcing on the other hand, may expose organizations to information, and safety hazards caused by lack of regulation. These hazards can in certain nations directly result from work ethics that are substandard or diverse. For example, in several Asian countries copyrighted software is exchanged, a practice banned in Europe and other developed nations. IT organizations involved in offshore outsourcing have to take care of the vulnerability and security of its internal and customer data in terms of legal, ethics or business responsibilities.[66] Therefore, IT companies should consider the track record of the candidate country and/or service provider to shield themselves against information safety problems. Their privacy-, information release-, and safety-regulations should be analyzed.[67]

Socio-cultural problems: Cultural differences might cause the misunderstanding of business talks and professional conduct. In determining where to outsource, corporations have to take responsibility for the national orientation of their personnel and the cultural standards of externally sourced workforce.[68] Countries without a business spirit and a propensity to flourish would not do well in the competitive world economy. Governments without a vision for international business might bring significant disadvantages to any

---

[64] cf. *Hirschheim, R., Heinzl, A., Dibbern, J.,* Information Systems Outsourcing, 2020, p. 346.
[65] cf. *Hirschheim, R., Heinzl, A., Dibbern, J.,* Information Systems Outsourcing, 2020, p. 313f.
[66] cf. *Hirschheim, R., Heinzl, A., Dibbern, J.,* Information Systems Outsourcing, 2020, p. 12 f.
[67] cf. *Djavanshir, G.,* Surveying the risks and benefits of IT outsourcing, 2005, p. 254.
[68] cf. *Hirschheim, R., Heinzl, A., Dibbern, J.,* Information Systems Outsourcing, 2020, p. 11f.

company that attempts to engage in business. Special interest groups such as student organisations, labor unions or religious organizations in some nations may wish to impede the activities of a foreign corporation. This blockage may potentially constitute a risk source.[69]

Immature business environment: Different dimensions manifest themselves in the immaturity of business environments, including volatile currency exchanges, weak national currencies, high foreign corporate taxes, high import and export tariffs, rigid customs legislation and regulations which deter foreign companies. Countries without an affordable and reliable broadband telecommunications infrastructure can, for instance, be challenging to manage. The lack of commitment to modern business standards and processes is another sign of an immature company environment. Product development in such a country can lead to poor design since IT vendors are not up-to-date on current and ongoing technology.[70]

4 Conclusion

In summary, it can be said that the outsourcing of IT services is increasingly becoming standard practice in today's IT world. As the previous chapters have shown, the practice of outsourcing offers many advantages and opportunities. However, these in turn are also accompanied by potential disadvantages. Corporate and product-specific applications and forms of outsourcing can vary greatly, making it difficult to give a definite answer to the question of a general benefit of outsourcing. It is therefore necessary to consider within the specific use cases whether and how outsourcing of IT services is practicable or not.

---

[69] cf. *Djavanshir, G.*, Surveying the risks and benefits of IT outsourcing, 2005, p. 37.
[70] cf. *Djavanshir, G.*, Surveying the risks and benefits of IT outsourcing, 2005, p. 36-37.

Bibliography

Amberg, Michael, Wiener, Martin (IT-Offshoring, 2006): IT-Offshoring: Management internationaler IT-Outsourcing-Projekte, Heidelberg: Physica-Verlag, 2006
Aubert, B.A., Dussault, S., Patry, M., Rivard, S. (Managing the risk of IT outsourcing, 1999): Managing the risk of IT outsourcing, 1st ed., Hawaii: HICSS, 1999, 10 pp.

Beulen, Erik, Ribbers, Pieter, Roos, Jan (Managing IT Outsourcing, 2006): Managing IT Outsourcing, London: Routledge, 2006

Deering, Andre (Outsourcing, 2015): Outsourcing: Strategies, Challenges and Effects on Organizations, Hauppauge, New York: Nova Science Publishers, Inc, 2015
Djavanshir, G.R. (Surveying the risks and benefits of IT outsourcing, 2005): Surveying the risks and benefits of IT outsourcing, 7th ed., IT Professional, 2005, pp. 32–37

Georg Hodosi, Lazar Rusu (Risks, Relationships and Success Factors in IT Outsourcing, 2019): Risks, Relationships and Success Factors in IT Outsourcing: A Study in Large Companies, 1st ed., Switzerland: Springer International Publishing, 2019

Hagen, Rickmann, Stefan, Diefenbach, Kai T., Brüning (IT-Outsourcing, 2013): IT-Outsourcing: Neue Herausforderungen im Zeitalter von Cloud Computing, Berlin: Springer, 2013
Hirschheim, Rudy, Heinzl, Armin, Dibbern, Jens (Information Systems Outsourcing, 2020): Information Systems Outsourcing: The Era of Digital Transformation, 5th ed., Switzerland: Springer International Publishing, 2020

Laplante, P.A., Costello, T., Singh, Pawan, Bindiganavile, Sudi, Landon, M. (The who, what, why, where, and when of IT outsourcing, 2004): The who, what, why, where, and when of IT outsourcing, 1st ed., IT Professional, 2004, pp. 19–23
Lux, Wolfgang, Schön, Peter (Outsourcing der Datenverarbeitung, 2012): Outsourcing der Datenverarbeitung: von der Idee zur Umsetzung, 2nd ed., Heidelberg: Springer, 2012

Picot, Arnold, Maier, Matthias (Anaylse- und Gestaltungskonzepte für das Outsourcing, 1993): in Scheer: Rechnungswesen und EDV: Controlling bei fließenden Unternehmensstrukturen, Heidelberg: Physica-Verlag, 1993

Rost, Johann (The Insider's Guide to Outsourcing Risks and Rewards, 2006): The Insider's Guide to Outsourcing Risks and Rewards, 1st ed., New York: Auerbach Publications (CRC Press), 2006

Schwarze, Lars, Müller, Peter (IT-Outsourcing – Erfahrungen, 2005): IT-Outsourcing - Erfahrungen, Status und zukünftige Herausforderungen. In: HMD - Praxis Wirtschaftsinform. 245 (2005)

Söbbing, Thomas (Handbuch IT-Outsourcing, 2002): Handbuch IT-Outsourcing: Rechtlich, strategische und steuerliche Fragen, Bonn: mitp-Verlag, 2002

Vorontsova, Anna, Rusu, Lazar (Determinants of IT Outsourcing Relationships, 2014): Determinants of IT Outsourcing Relationships: A Recipient – Provider Perspective, 16th ed., Sweden: Procedia Technology, 2014, pp. 588–597

Walters, B., Tang, Z. (IT-Enabled Strategic Management, 2006): IT-Enabled Strategic Management: Increasing Returns for the Organization, London: Idea Group Publishing, 2006

Internet sources

CNBC (Salesforces 'major issue' with its cloud service, 2019): Salesforce says a 'major issue' with its cloud service results in outage for some customers, [Online; accessed July 23, 2021], <https://www.cnbc.com/2019/05/17/salesforce-says-a-major-issue-with-cloud-service-results-in-downtime.html> (2019)

Future Processing Start Nearshoring (IT outsourcing lifecycle, 2021): IT outsourcing lifecycle, [Online; accessed July 24, 2021], <https://startnearshoring.com/wp-content/uploads/2018/01/IT_outsourcing_lifecycle_photo.png> (2021)

Statista (Public Cloud Revenue by Segment, 2021): Public Cloud Revenue by Segment, [Online; accessed July 25, 2021], <https://www.statista.com/outlook/tmo/public-cloud/worldwide#revenue> (2021)

YOUR KNOWLEDGE HAS VALUE